P9-DFS-945

JAMES
BEARD'S
SHELLFISH

JAMES BEARD'S
SHELLFISH

EDITED BY JOHN FERRONE

THAMES AND HUDSON
NEW YORK, NEW YORK

James Beard's recipes and text are adapted from previously published material and are used by permission of Reed College and the executors of his will.

Copyright ©1997 by John Ferrone

First published in the United States of America in paperback in 1997 by Thames and Hudson Inc., 500 Fifth Avenue, New York, New York, 10110

Library of Congress Catalog Card Number 97–60238
ISBN 0–500–27967–5

All rights reserved. No part of this publication may be reproduced or transmitted in any form or by any means, electronic or mechanical, including photocopy, recording, or any other information storage and retrieval system, without prior permission in writing from the publisher.

Designed, typeset and produced by Liz Trovato Book Design
Cover illustration by Patricia Pardini

Printed and bound in Mexico

EDITOR'S NOTE

All of the recipes and much of the text in this cookbook series are James Beard's and are gathered from many sources—magazine articles, syndicated columns, cookbooks, cooking lessons—covering thirty years of culinary exploration. The choice of recipes gives a fair sampling of his thinking on a variety of foods and cuisines. Although he is associated primarily with American cookery, Beard was always on the lookout for gastronomic inspiration in other parts of the world. These cookbooks offer dishes from Portland to Paris, from Maryland to Mexico. Many of them are Beard favorites that turned up in his cooking classes and cookbooks through the years, but also included are less familiar dishes that deserve to be better known. Recipes and text have been edited for these special editions.

BEARD ON SHELLFISH

I can't think of a time when I haven't loved seafood. Some of my earliest memories center around crab pools in my native Oregon. As the tide receded, shallow pools formed, and in those days, before mass fishing took over, the unsuspecting Dungeness crabs would hide in the sands rather than retreat out to sea. We would forage in the pools armed with rakes—or just our bare hands—and pull out any number of these formidable-looking creatures. When we had a good haul, we would carry them home to be cooked in seawater or salted flavored water of our own concocting.

There's an art to removing the prized leg meat from a Dungeness crab. First the claws must be cracked and the shells cut with sharp scissors or a knife; then the delectable leg meat can be taken out in one beautiful piece. Whenever we had visitors from the Eastern United States or Europe we would proudly serve these crab legs as something very much of our own Northwest.

We also rejoiced in an abundance of the delicate river crayfish—not the priceless luxury then that they are today. We would trek up the Necanicum River from our beach settlement with a basket, pieces of string, and calf's liver, which, when lowered on the string, attracted vast numbers of these little shellfish. We cooked them in red wine with spices and herbs. Cold crayfish with homemade bread and sweet butter and wine or beer makes one of the finest feasts I know.

With all this bounty ours for the taking, we didn't miss the Eastern lobster, which, in any case, only came to us canned because of the problems of transportation. Consequently, it was not until I went to Europe to study that I became acquainted with lobster. Perhaps it is because my taste for it developed so much later, when my loyalty to crab and the tiny bay shrimps was already entrenched, that I felt I could live without it.

I have eaten and cooked a lot of lobster in my lifetime, and my respect and appetite for this remarkable shellfish has increased, but I would still trade a whole catch of lobsters for a good Dungeness crab.   Nowadays, when Maine lobsters can be had all over the country and even Dungeness crab has found its way to many outlying spots, I must confess to a wistful longing for the old days when one ate such foods only in their native habitat and in the native ways. Much of the fun and excitement is lost when you can pick up a menu and order the same lobster dishes in California as in Damariscotta, Maine, or find a crab specialty in Dayton that once you could enjoy only in Seattle or San Francisco. That, I suppose, is what we mean by progress.

JAMES BEARD

CONTENTS

Shrimp

Crab

Lobster

Oysters and Clams

Scallops and Other Shellfish

SHRIMP

BEARD ON SHRIMP

No other shellfish even approaches shrimp in popularity. You can find cooked or raw shrimp in supermarkets in the smallest villages as well as in fish markets in big cities. Shrimp, especially the ubiquitous shrimp cocktail (with a sometimes pretty badly flavored sauce that I have heard called "the red menace"), has become one of the more staple ingredients of American cuisine. In restaurants across the country you can order shrimp cocktail, shrimp salad, broiled shrimp, and shrimp masquerading under the name of "scampi," which they are not. The shrimp we eat comes from all over the world—from Panama, the Indian Ocean, France, Denmark, and Norway as well as from our own Atlantic and Pacific waters and the Gulf of Mexico. Still, all too few people know the delights of the very tiny shrimp from the coasts of Alaska, Maine, California, and Oregon, as delicate and delicious as any seafood can be. If you buy these shrimp (the French call them *crevette rose*) in the shell with the heads on, they are great for a cocktail party. Just put out a huge pile of cooked shrimp and let everyone shell for himself.

There are two vital points to remember when cooking shrimp. First, there is no reason to ruin the taste and texture by overcooking, no matter how large they are. Plunge them into rapidly boiling salted water, and after it returns to the boil give them no more than 3 to 5 minutes, according to size (for the tiny shrimp, 1 minute is enough), then drain immediately. Second, always salt the water well; otherwise you won't get a good-tasting shrimp.

Before you cook shrimp, it is a good idea to remove the dark intestinal vein running along the back, although the Shrimp Association says there is no reason save aesthetics to do so. It certainly won't harm you if you don't. You can easily remove the vein when you peel the shrimp by cutting through the curve of the shell with scissors and washing the vein out.

STUFFED BROILED SHRIMP

The West Coast food authority Helen Evans Brown created this simple but unusual treatment of shrimp.

3 to 5 large cooked and shelled shrimp per person
Flat anchovy fillets
Bacon slices, cut in half

Slice each shrimp almost in half. Lay an anchovy fillet between the halves, close, and wrap with a bacon slice. Arrange on skewers, and broil just until the bacon is crisp.

TEMPURA

Serves 6

The secret of these Japanese-style shrimp is in the beer batter, which gives a casing that is both crisp and light. The other essential is a high enough temperature for the oil, or else these delectable shrimp can turn soggy.

Oil for deep-frying
2 pounds shrimp, shelled and
*   deveined, with tail shells intact*
2 eggs, separated
¾ cup beer
1 tablespoon olive oil
1 cup sifted flour
1 tablespoon soy sauce
1 teaspoon dry mustard
Additional flour

Heat oil in a deep fryer to slightly over 365°. Beat the egg yolks with the beer, oil, flour, soy sauce, and mustard to make a well-blended batter. Beat the egg whites until firm and fold into the batter. Let the batter rest 1 hour or longer. Dip the shrimp in flour and then into the batter. Lower them by spoon into the frying basket, a few at a time, and cook for 3 to 4 minutes. Make sure the temperature remains at 365° or above for each batch. Drain on paper towels. Serve with soy sauce and hot mustard.

LIZ LUCAS SHRIMP

Serves 10 to 12

Marinated with the simple flavors of lemon and onion, these shrimp make a refreshing first course, buffet dish or nibble with drinks.

3 pounds cooked and shelled shrimp
3 medium onions thinly sliced
3 or 4 lemons thinly sliced
Chopped parsley
Salt and freshly ground black pepper
¼ teaspoon Tabasco
Olive oil
3 bay leaves

Make layers of shrimp, onion slices, lemon slices, and parsley in a deep serving dish. Add the seasonings and olive oil to cover. (If you have cooked the shrimp in well-salted water, you may need very little seasoning.) Top with the bay leaves. Refrigerate 6 to 8 hours or overnight to marinate. Arrange on a bed of greens.

SPINACH ROLL WITH SHRIMP FILLING

A good luncheon dish, this is actually a spinach soufflé baked in a jelly-roll pan. While it is not hard to make, it looks and tastes delicious.

3 pounds fresh or 4 packages frozen
  spinach
6 tablespoons melted butter
Salt and freshly ground black pepper
2 to 3 dashes nutmeg
4 eggs, separated
¼ cup fine dry bread crumbs
2 tablespoons grated Parmesan cheese
⅔ cup onions or green onions,
  finely chopped
4 tablespoons butter
3 tablespoons flour
½ cup dry vermouth or dry white wine
Dash Tabasco
1 tablespoon fresh tarragon, chopped,
  or 1 teaspoon dried
1½ cups light cream
½ cup parsley, chopped
1½ to 2 cups cooked and shelled
  tiny shrimp

Fresh spinach should be washed and placed in a kettle with no water other than that clinging to the leaves, tightly covered, and wilted over medium heat, which only takes a few minutes. Drain well and chop coarsely. Thaw frozen spinach in a pan over very gentle heat or pour boiling water over it. Drain extremely well, since frozen spinach has a high water content.

Place the chopped spinach in a bowl, and mix in the melted butter, 1½ teaspoons of salt, ½ teaspoon of freshly ground black pepper, and the nutmeg. Beat in the egg yolks one at a time. Then beat the egg whites until they hold soft peaks and fold into the mixture.

Butter an 11-by-14-inch jelly-roll pan, line it with waxed paper or cooking parchment, and butter that also. Sprinkle with the bread crumbs. Spread the spinach mixture evenly in the pan, sprinkle with the Parmesan and bake in a 350° oven for about 15 minutes.

Meanwhile lightly sauté the onions or green onions in the 4 tablespoons of butter until just limp. Blend in the flour, and cook for a minute or so. Mix in the vermouth or wine, and season with ½ teaspoon salt and ½ teaspoon freshly ground black pepper. Add the Tabasco and tarragon, and stir in the cream. Continue stirring until nicely thickened. Taste for seasoning. Then add the parsley and shrimp and mix gently.

Remove the cooked spinach roll from the oven and invert on a length of buttered foil. Peel off the waxed paper. Spread with two-thirds of the shrimp mixture, then carefully roll up by lifting the edge of the foil, and roll onto a serving dish. Spoon the remaining shrimp mixture over it, and serve.

GRILLED OR BROILED SHRIMP

Serves 4

2 pounds large (about 8 per pound)
   shrimp
1 cup olive oil
1 cup dry white wine or dry vermouth
2 cloves of garlic, finely chopped
1 teaspoon salt
1 teaspoon freshly ground black pepper
¼ cup parsley, finely chopped

Slit the back of each shrimp and remove the shell, leaving the tail intact. Also remove the dark intestinal vein. Mix the rest of the ingredients together in a bowl, add the shrimp, and turn to coat thoroughly. Allow to marinate for at least 2 hours, turning several more times.

Drain and arrange in a basket grill or on skewers. Grill over coals or under a broiler for about 5 minutes, turning once and brushing with the marinade.

DIETER'S SHRIMP AND CRABMEAT SALAD

Serves 6

If your low-calorie diet is also salt-free, don't try to get something to taste like salt—nothing does. One must stimulate the palate with other flavors, like garlic, herbs, well-flavored vinegars, and fresh pepper.

1½ pounds large shrimp
1 pound crabmeat
2 garlic cloves
4 sprigs of parsley
4 teaspoons fresh tarragon, chopped
1 cup dry white wine
4 tablespoons sherry wine vinegar
4 medium carrots, peeled and shredded
1 large onion, peeled and finely chopped
1 tablespoon fresh chervil, chopped
¼ cup parsley, chopped
Freshly ground black pepper
4 tablespoons olive oil
Yogurt
Salad greens
Cherry tomatoes

Split the shrimp down the back and remove the intestinal veins and the shells, leaving the tails intact. Pour 1 quart of water into a pan, and add the garlic, parsley sprigs, 1 teaspoon of the tarragon, the wine, and 2 tablespoons of the vinegar. Bring to a boil, and cook 5 minutes. Add the shrimp, return to a boil, and cook for 3 minutes. Drain and allow the shrimp to cool.

In a large bowl mix together the carrots, onion, chervil, chopped parsley, and remaining tarragon and vinegar. Toss with the crabmeat. Sprinkle with freshly ground black pepper to taste. Add the oil and just enough yogurt to bind the salad. Arrange on a bed of salad greens, and garnish with the shrimp and cherry tomatoes.

POTTED SHRIMP

Serves 4

Potted Shrimp originated in England and is as commonly served there as shrimp cocktail is in the United States. It has a buttery, spicy quality that is quite addictive. You can make it with tiny shelled canned or frozen shrimp, but it is infinitely better with fresh ones, cooked about 1 minute in boiling salted water.

1 pound cooked and shelled tiny shrimp
8 ounces clarified butter
¼ teaspoon freshly grated nutmeg
Pinch of cayenne pepper

Toss the shrimp in about 6 ounces of the hot, clear butter, and add the seasonings. Ladle the shrimp into small pots. Seal each pot with a thin layer of the remaining butter. Allow to cool, then chill in the refrigerator. Will keep for about a week. Serve with cocktails or as a first course with thinly sliced buttered brown bread or homemade Melba toast.

CRAB

BEARD ON CRAB

Crabs vary so much around the shorelines of the United States that, although the different crab meats are really interchangeable, admirers of this succulent crustacean tend to favor the local product. The palate of the West Coaster, where the Dungeness crab reigns, seldom finds the same satisfaction in crab from other parts of the country. Marylanders swear by their blue crab, whereas Alaskans prefer to feast on the king crab and the Dungeness, both of which abound in their waters, and Floridians in the southernmost reaches enjoy the claws of the stone crab

Soft-shelled crabs or buster crabs are not a different variety of crab, but merely the Eastern blue crab caught as it molts or "busts" its old shell and eaten before the brand-new soft shell has had a chance to harden. The soft-shelled crabs sold in markets are cleaned and ready to cook whole— sautéing and broiling are the most usual methods. The smaller soft-shelled crabs are best for eating. Allow 2 or 3 per serving.

Dungeness crab is usually bought cooked in the shell, which is then cracked so that the leg and back meat can be extracted. Unlike that of the Eastern crab, the large leg meat of this crab is considered the best part. The huge king crab is removed from the shell before cooking and eating, because of the size of the shells and the pieces of meat. Stone crab claws are usually served in the shell, hot or cold, to be eaten with picks and small forks.

SAUTÉED CRAB WITH HAM

A simple and delicious marriage of the flavors of Maryland crab and Virginia ham. It can, of course, be made with Dungeness crab, from the West Coast, or any other good lump crabmeat.

FOR EACH SERVING:

⅓ pound lump crabmeat

2 tablespoons butter

Lemon juice

Salt and freshly ground black pepper

1 teaspoon grated or finely
    chopped onion

Dash of Tabasco

Pinch fresh thyme or savory, chopped

Thin slices Smithfield or other
    good Virginia ham

For best results each serving should be cooked in a small individual skillet with a lid. Otherwise, several servings can be arranged in one large skillet. Sauté the crabmeat in the butter until just heated through, then add a squeeze of lemon juice, a sprinkling of salt and pepper, the grated onion, Tabasco, and thyme or savory. Cover with paper-thin slices of ham, put the lid on, and simmer for 2 or 3 minutes until the ham is slightly curled at the edges. Serve as is or on toast.

CURRIED CRABMEAT CRÊPES

You can fill crêpes with almost anything you might normally serve on toast or over rice. Crêpes just make it taste better, as is true of this recipe.

2 pounds crabmeat
6 tablespoons butter
2 tablespoons vegetable oil
1 small onion or 6 shallots, chopped
2 pimientos, chopped
4 tablespoons flour
2 teaspoons curry powder
1 cup milk
¼ cup cognac
2 tablespoons chopped parsley
12 unsweetened crêpes

Sauté the onion or shallots in 2 tablespoons of butter and the oil until lightly browned. Add the pimientos and crabmeat and cook 2 to 3 minutes or until heated through. Transfer to a bowl. Melt the remaining butter in a saucepan, blend in the flour and curry powder, and cook over medium heat for a minute or so. Gradually stir in the milk and the cognac. Cook until smooth. Add the crabmeat and parsley. Put a dollop of the mixture on each of the crêpes and roll them up. Arrange in a shallow buttered baking dish, seam side down, and just heat through in a 375° oven.

CRÊPES (UNSWEETENED)

1 cup less 1 tablespoon all-purpose
   flour
⅛ teaspoon salt
3 eggs
2 tablespoons melted butter
1½ cups milk

Sift the flour and salt into a bowl. Add the eggs, one at a time, and mix thoroughly to make a smooth batter. Stir in the melted butter, and then gradually stir in the milk. The batter should be as runny as thin cream. Allow it to rest for at least an hour.

Butter a 6-inch crêpe pan, and place over medium-high heat. When the pan is hot pour in just enough batter to form a thin, even coating. When bubbles begin to form on the surface, lift one end of the crêpe with a spatula to see if it is lightly browned. Then turn the crêpe to brown on the other side. Transfer to a warm plate and keep hot while you bake the rest of the crêpes. Makes about 18 crêpes.

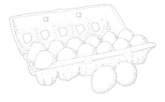

CRABMEAT CHARENTAIS

Serves 4

A close cousin of this dish, minus the green pepper, was long a favorite at the Four Seasons restaurant in New York, where it was prepared at tableside in a chafing dish, under the name Crabmeat Casanova. It makes an elegant first course.

1 pound crabmeat
4 thin slices French bread
6 tablespoons butter
3 or 4 green onions, finely sliced,
*   or ¼ cup finely chopped shallots*
1 small green pepper, finely chopped
1 tablespoon grated carrot
⅓ cup white wine
Salt and freshly ground black pepper
1½ teaspoons chopped fresh tar-
*   ragon or ½ teaspoon dried*
⅓ cup cognac
Lemon slices
Chopped parsley

In a skillet brown the bread slices quickly in 4 tablespoons of the butter, and transfer them to a hot platter. Add the remaining butter to the pan and cook the green onions, pepper and carrot over brisk heat for 2 minutes. Add the white wine, crab and seasonings, and toss lightly until the crab is heated through. Heat the cognac, ignite, and pour over the crab. Toss again to blend in the cognac. Spoon over the bread, and garnish with lemon slices and chopped parsley.

CRAB MARTINIQUAIS

Serves 6

A dish that has traveled from the West Indies by way of a French kitchen.

1 pound crabmeat

6 strips of bacon, diced

2 medium onions, finely chopped

1 clove garlic, finely chopped

½ pound smoked ham, cut in
    thin strips

3 tablespoons tomato paste

⅓ cup dark rum

1 cup white wine

Pinch of sugar

Salt

Freshly ground black pepper

1 tablespoon chopped parsley

⅓ cup heavy cream

Cook the bacon in a skillet until barely crisp. Add the onion and garlic and cook until just beginning to color. Add the ham and heat through. Then add the tomato paste and crabmeat. Pour the rum over this, and ignite. Add the wine, parsley, sugar and salt and pepper to taste. Simmer about 15 minutes. Stir in heavy cream and cook for another 2 to 3 minutes. Serve with plain boiled rice or a rice pilaf.

WEST COAST CRAB CAKES

Serves 4 to 6

A novel version of crab cakes, originating in San Francisco, that owes its accents to Asian cookery.

1 pound crabmeat
1 pound cooked fish, flaked
8 water chestnuts, finely chopped
6 to 8 green onions, finely sliced
2 egg yolks
½ teaspoon salt
¼ teaspoon freshly ground black
   pepper
5 tablespoons vegetable oil
2 tablespoons chopped fresh coriander
Soy sauce

Combine the crabmeat, flaked fish, water chestnuts, green onions, egg yolks, and salt and pepper in a bowl. Blend well and form into 8 patties. Sauté slowly in the oil in a large skillet, turning once, until lightly browned on both sides. Do not overcook. Drain on paper towels. Sprinkle with coriander and serve with soy sauce.

SOFT-SHELLED CRABS
SAUTÉ MEUNIÈRE

Soft-shelled crabs or buster crabs are simply Eastern blue crabs that have molted or "busted" their old shells. They are caught and eaten before the new shells have hardened. They are sold cleaned and ready to cook. The smaller the better.

2 to 3 small soft-shelled crabs per serving
Flour
1 tablespoon butter per crab
Salt and freshly ground black pepper
Chopped parsley
Lemon wedges

Dip the crabs in flour and sauté them on both sides over medium heat until they are crisp. Season with salt and pepper as they cook. Remove the crabs to a hot serving dish and spoon the pan juices over them. Sprinkle with chopped parsley and serve with lemon wedges. The entire crab can be eaten.

CRAB DIABLE PRUNIER

Serves 4

This is a recipe inspired by the famous family-run Prunier restaurant, which had establishments in Paris and London and specialized in fish and shellfish dishes.

1 pound crabmeat
1 small onion, finely chopped
2 shallots, finely chopped
4 tablespoons butter
¼ cup cognac or brandy
2 teaspoons Dijon mustard
1½ cups rich béchamel sauce (using part cream and part milk)
Buttered bread crumbs
Chopped parsley

Sauté the onion and shallots in the butter until limp and just beginning to color. Rinse the pan with the cognac over low heat, then stir in the mustard and white sauce. Stir in the crabmeat. Taste for seasoning. Divide among 4 ovenproof dishes, sprinkle with the buttered crumbs and parsley, and heat in a 425° oven just long enough to lightly brown the crumbs.

LOBSTER

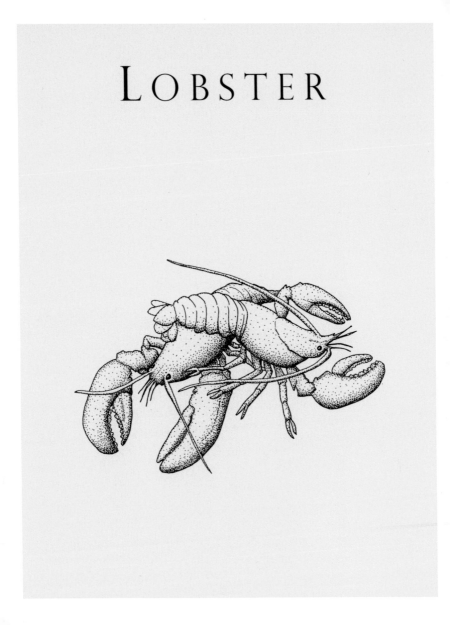

BEARD ON LOBSTER

Lobsters abound in East Coast waters from Long Island to far north in Canada, although they are not as plentiful off the Massachusetts and Maine coasts as they used to be. Lobsters are sold in different sizes, all the way up from the delicate little 1-pound ones called "chicken" lobsters, which yield 4 or 5 ounces of meat, to enormous monsters weighing up to 20 or 25 pounds. These heavy ones make exceedingly good eating, but you won't find them very often.

If you live far away from lobster country, there are several lobster farms in Maine and Canada that will air-ship lobsters packed in seaweed alive and kicking. Not everyone is prepared to deal with an active lobster. If you are squeamish about plunging one into boiling water, put it in cold water, cover the pot, and bring the water to a full boil so the lobster just wafts away in a dreamy state. Otherwise, grasp the lobster behind the head, slip it head first into boiling salted water, cover the pot and after the water returns to a boil cook it for 5 minutes for the first pound and about 3 minutes for every additional pound. Remove from the water at once and let it cool if you are serving it cold. If you are serving it hot, split it lengthwise and remove the dark intestinal vein that runs down the center of the tail. Reserve the greenish tomalley and any coral.

For broiling, the live lobster must be split before cooking. First make a deep incision with the point of a heavy knife where the head and body meet, severing the spinal cord. Then cut right through the entire length of the lobster with knife and mallet or with shears. Drain it, and remove the vein and stomach. Again, reserve the greenish tomalley and coral.

When you serve hot lobster, supply large napkins or bibs, shears, lobster crackers, picks for getting the meat from the claws, plenty of melted butter and lemon, good bread, and either cold beer or chilled white wine.

LOBSTER À LA NAGE
(IN COURT BOUILLON)

A superb variation on plain boiled lobster. Lobster cooked this way is also delicious cold, served with a brisk mustard mayonnaise combined with chopped capers and finely chopped fresh dill.

2 lobsters weighing 1½ pounds each
1 large onion, thinly sliced
4 tablespoons butter
1 large carrot, cut into rounds
2 or 3 shallots, finely chopped
3 or 4 parsley sprigs

FOR THE COURT BULLION:
Bottle of dry white wine
3½ cups water
1 tablespoon salt
1 bay leaf
1 teaspoon dried thyme

In a heavy skillet sauté the onion slices until just wilted. Add the carrot, shallots, and parsley and cook for a minute. Transfer to a pan or kettle large enough to accommodate the lobsters. Add the wine, water, salt, and herbs. Bring to a boil, cover, and simmer for 25 minutes. Plunge the lobsters into this court bouillon, bring the liquid back to a boil, and simmer for about 8 minutes.

Remove the lobsters, cut off the claws and crack them, and split the lobsters lengthwise. Serve them in deep dishes in the court bouillon with plenty of French bread and butter and a good Alsatian Riesling.

LOBSTER DROUANT

Serves 4

A rich, highly seasoned treatment of lobster that originated in a Parisian seafood restaurant.

4 small or 2 large lobsters
Melted butter
2½ cups Sauce Suprême (see below)
1 tablespoon dry mustard
Cayenne
1 cup grated Switzerland Swiss cheese

Split the live lobsters, and remove the intestinal tracts. Brush the meat lightly with butter, and broil, cut side up, for 15 to 18 minutes, depending on the size of the lobsters. Remove the meat, and reserve the shells. Cut the meat crosswise into scallops about ½ inch thick, and remove the meat from the claws.

Season the Sauce Suprême with the dry mustard and a few grains of cayenne. Spread a thin layer in the shells. Fill with the pieces of lobster. Cover with the rest of the sauce, sprinkle with the grated cheese, and bake in a 400° oven until the cheese is melted and lightly browned.

SAUCE SUPRÊME

2 tablespoons butter
2 tablespoons flour
1 cup chicken broth
Salt, if needed
Freshly ground black pepper
Pinch freshly grated nutmeg
3 egg yolks
1 cup heavy cream

Melt the butter in a small heavy saucepan, stir in the flour, and cook over moderate heat for 2 or 3 minutes, while continuing to stir. Gradually add the chicken broth, and cook until smooth and thickened. Taste for salt. Add a light grind of pepper and nutmeg. Beat the egg yolks lightly and combine with the cream. Stir a spoonful or two of the hot sauce into the egg-cream mixture to temper it, and then stir this back into the sauce. Cook over low heat until just hot through, but do not allow to boil.

BAKED LOBSTER PROVENÇAL

A long-time Beard favorite because of its simple but pleasing combination of flavors.

FOR EACH SERVING:

1½-pound lobster, boiled and cooled
1 garlic clove, finely chopped
3 tablespoons olive oil
2 tablespoons chopped parsley
1 teaspoon or more of lemon juice
Salt and freshly ground black
   pepper to taste
Butter
Buttered bread crumbs

Split the lobster, crack the claws, and remove the body and claw meat, the tomalley, and the coral, if there is any. Clean and reserve the shells. Chop the meat quite fine and blend in the garlic, olive oil, parsley, lemon juice, and salt and pepper, along with the tomalley and any coral.

Butter the lobster shells and stuff them with the lobster mixture. Sprinkle with buttered bread crumbs, dot with butter, and arrange on a rack in a shallow baking pan. Bake at 350° until the lobster is heated through and the crumbs are delicately browned, about 20 minutes.

Drink a good Chablis with this.

LOBSTER AND CELERY ROOT SALAD

Serves 4

Lobster makes the most luxurious of salads and doesn't require any dressing up, but celery root provides a welcome complement of flavor and texture.

2 cups diced cooked lobster meat
1 cup raw celery root cut in fine
    strips (julienne)
Rémoulade sauce
Greens
Hard-boiled eggs, quartered

RÉMOULADE SAUCE:
1 1/2 cups mayonnaise
1 hard-boiled egg, finely chopped
2 tablespoons finely chopped capers
1 tablespoon finely chopped parsley
A few drops of lemon juice
Salt and freshly ground black
    pepper to taste

Blend the lobster and celery root with just enough rémoulade sauce to bind the ingredients.

Arrange on lettuce leaves of your choice, and garnish with the eggs.

OYSTERS AND CLAMS

BEARD ON OYSTERS AND CLAMS

Oysters vary in size, looks and taste because the water, climate and even the exact location of an oyster bed have profound effects on their growth. They range from plump and grayish with a bland taste, to greenish or even coppery with a definite metallic taste. Some are as small as your fingernail and others, such as the Japanese or the Malpeques from Prince Edward Island, as big or bigger than the palm of your hand. The Pacific Northwest, where I grew up, is noted for its tiny Olympia oysters from Puget Sound. An oyster lover can consume at least 250 at a sitting. They command a premium price. On the East Coast, the Chincoteagues from Chesapeake Bay are the nearest to the Olympias.

Cape Cod oysters were probably the first to attain popularity in America. We also have had oysters from Delaware Bay—Philadelphians are great oyster fans to this day—and the famous Lynnhavens from the waters of Virginia, although they are no longer easy to come by. New Orleans oysters have been famed since the city was founded, and the local cuisine boasts many oyster specialties, among them the well-known Oysters Rockefeller.

America is well supplied with clams and likes them better than do other countries. They come in so many varieties, especially on the Pacific Coast, that it is difficult for an inlander to remember which is which. The two main East Coast species are the soft or long-necked clam and the hard or little-necked clam, known to New Englanders as the "quahog." There are some thirty varieties on the Pacific Coast, including the razor—unsurpassed in flavor and texture—the Pismo, the mud clam, and the gargantuan geoduck. There are also a number of regional varieties, the best known of which is the "cherrystone"—a small quahog—popularly served on the half shell. Raw clams are best eaten with nothing but lemon juice and a little pepper or horseradish, and no drop of the delicious juice should be lost.

OYSTERS ON THE HALF SHELL

Most oyster fans insist that this delicacy is at its best served raw on the half shell. And in this form they need little or no embellishment. A dash of lemon juice and maybe a touch of freshly ground black pepper. But no vinegar, no chili sauce and no cocktail sauce. With them serve thin sandwiches of buttered rye bread and a good white wine such as Chablis or Pouilly-Fuissé or beer or stout.

Here are some ways to vary oysters on the half shell:

• Serve with lemon juice and black pepper and piping hot grilled or sautéed pork sausages; or with slices of garlic sausage. Be sure the sausages are hot and served on a hot plate and the oysters freshly opened and well chilled.

• For a glamorous party dish, serve oysters on a bed of ice with a dab of fresh caviar and a squirt of lemon juice atop each one.

• Serve with lemon juice and black pepper, and pass bowls of chopped chives and parsley.

• With cocktails pass large trays of the oysters with lemon quarters, caviar, if you like, and piping hot tiny sausages.

PUREE OF OYSTER SOUP

Serves 6

A delicious departure from the usual oyster stew.

18 shucked oysters
1 quart bottled clam juice
½ cup rice
4 tablespoons butter
Salt
Freshly ground black pepper
¼ teaspoon Tabasco
1½ cups heavy cream
¼ cup cognac
Chopped parsley

Bring the clam juice to a simmer in a saucepan, add the rice, and cook until very soft, about 45 minutes. Stir in the butter, then force through a sieve or put in a blender or food processor to puree the rice. Return to the saucepan. Chop 12 of the oysters and puree with their liquid. Add to the clam juice–rice mixture.

Add the Tabasco and heavy cream. Season with salt and pepper to taste. Bring to the boiling point. Add the 6 whole oysters and cook just until the edges curl. Add the cognac and cook 2 minutes longer. Ladle into soup cups or bowls, and put a whole oyster in each. Garnish with chopped parsley.

DEEP-FRIED OYSTERS

Serves 4

Also called "French-fried." Fry no more than 4 or 5 of these delicious nuggets at a time, to keep them from touching each other, and serve them piping hot.

1 quart shucked oysters
Fat or oil for deep frying
2 eggs
3 tablespoons cream
1 teaspoon salt
*½ teaspoon freshly ground black
    pepper*
Flour
*Bread crumbs, cracker crumbs or
    cornmeal*

Heat the fat or oil in a deep fryer to 380°. Meanwhile beat the eggs with the cream, and add the seasonings. Dip the oysters in the flour, then in the egg mixture, and finally in the crumbs. Fry for about 2 minutes. Drain on paper towels. Sprinkle with salt and pepper, and serve with lemon wedges.

VARIATION:

The oysters can also be fried in a skillet. Heat oil or fat to a depth of ½ inch until very hot. Drop in the prepared oysters a few at a time, and fry just a minute or two until the coating has browned.

OYSTERS CASENAVE

Serves 2

Called *"Huîtres Farcies"* by its French creator, this dish of oysters is not really stuffed but subtly anointed with an herbed butter.

FOR EACH 12 OYSTERS ON THE HALF SHELL:

6 shallots, finely chopped
½ cup chopped parsley
¼ cup chopped chervil
3 ounces butter, slightly softened
Salt
Freshly ground black pepper
Rock salt

Place the oysters on beds of rock salt in baking pans or shallow baking dishes. Blend the herbs with the softened butter, and top each oyster with a spoonful of the mixture. Sprinkle with salt and pepper. Bake in a 475° oven for 4 or 5 minutes or until the butter is melted and the edges of the oysters begin to curl.

OYSTERS CASINO

A dish that comes in many versions and in which the only constants are green pepper and bacon.

24 oysters on the half shell
½ cup butter
⅓ cup finely chopped shallots
¼ cup finely chopped parsley
¼ cup finely chopped green pepper
Lemon juice
6 slices bacon, cut in quarters and
    partially cooked

Place the oysters on beds of rock salt in baking pans or shallow baking dishes. Blend the butter with the shallots, parsley and green pepper. Put a spoonful of the mixture on each oyster and add a dash of lemon juice. Top with a piece of bacon. Bake in a 450° oven, or run under the broiler, just until the bacon is brown and the oysters are heated through.

OYSTERS EN BROCHETTE

An attractive and delicious way to serve oysters. It can be varied by the addition of other seafood, such as scallops and lobster meat.

FOR EACH BROCHETTE OR SKEWER:

4 shucked oysters

1 slice bacon, partially cooked and
*   cooled*

4 mushroom caps

Lemon juice

Freshly ground black pepper

Butter

Run the skewer through one end of the bacon, and add a mushroom cap and an oyster, then a loop of bacon and another mushroom cap and oyster, and so on, until the ingredients are used up. Sprinkle with lemon juice and a grind of pepper, and brush with butter. Broil over charcoal or in the broiler until the oysters are curled at the edges and the bacon is crisp.

OREGON CLAM CHOWDER

On the West Coast, especially the Northwest, where you have razor clams, the chowder is similar to the New England version, although at times light or heavy cream is used instead of milk, so this becomes a more formal soup. This is the Beard family recipe.

1½ cups chopped or ground fresh clams, preferably razor, with their liquor

3 slices salt pork or thick bacon slices

1 medium onion, finely chopped

2 medium potatoes, thinly sliced

3 cups light cream

Salt

Freshly ground black pepper

Butter

Thyme

Chopped parsley

This can be made with canned clams, if necessity bids. Drain the clams, and reserve the liquor. Cut the salt pork or bacon into small shreds, and cook in a skillet until crisp. Drain on paper towels. Cook the onion in the pork or bacon fat until beginning to color. Then cook the sliced potatoes in 2 cups boiling lightly salted water until tender. Add the bacon, onion, and clam liquor, and simmer 5 minutes. Add the light cream and bring to a boil. Season with salt, if needed, and pepper. Add the clams, and heat through. Pour into 4 to 6 bowls, and add a dollop of butter, a pinch of thyme and chopped parsley to each.

CLAMS AU GRATIN

Serves 6

Use smallish clams, such as cherrystones, for this dish.

36 clams on the half shell
½ cup finely chopped mushrooms
½ cup finely chopped shallots or
*   onion*
6 tablespoons butter
2 tablespoons finely chopped parsley
2 tablespoons finely chopped tomato
Salt
Freshly ground black pepper
⅓ to ½ cup dry bread crumbs

Place the clams in one large or two smaller baking pans. Sauté the mushrooms and shallots or onion in 4 tablespoons of the butter for 3 minutes or until the shallots begin to color. Add the parsley, tomato, and salt and pepper to taste. Spoon this over each of the clams, sprinkle with the crumbs, dot with butter, and bake at 400° for 5 to 8 minutes.

CLAM HASH

Clam Hash was a Beard family favorite during summers at the Oregon shore. It varied from meal to meal, but this was the general idea.

2 cups minced clams
6 tablespoons butter
1 tablespoon finely minced onion
1½ cups finely diced cooked potatoes
Salt to taste
Freshly ground black pepper
Nutmeg
4 egg yolks, well beaten
¼ cup grated Parmesan
6 tablespoons heavy cream

Melt the butter in a skillet and cook the onion until just tender. Add the clams and the potatoes, and mix to distribute them evenly, then press flat with a spatula. Season lightly with salt and pepper and a few grains of nutmeg. Cook for about 10 minutes over medium heat, then stir gently, turning up some of the bottom crust that has formed. Press flat again. Combine the beaten egg yolks with the grated cheese and cream, and pour over the hash. Cover and cook for a few minutes or until the egg mixture has set.

Turn out on a platter, and cut in wedges.

CLAM FRITTERS

Serves 4

2 eggs, separated
1 cup minced clams
1½ cups toasted bread crumbs or
    unsweetened cracker crumbs
½ teaspoon salt or more, to taste
Dash of Tabasco
Clam juice or milk, or a mixture
    of both

Beat the yolks until light. Add the minced clams, crumbs, salt, Tabasco and just enough clam juice or milk to make a heavy batter. Beat the egg whites until soft peaks form, and fold into the batter. Drop by spoonfuls onto a heated, well-buttered griddle or heavy skillet. Cook slowly until brown on the bottom, then turn and brown on the other side. Serve with a tartar sauce.

COLD CLAM BISQUE

An unusual addition to the repertoire of cold soups for the summer months.

1 pint shucked cherrystone or
    razor clams
½ cup rice
1 quart clam broth
3 tablespoons butter
Salt
Freshly ground black pepper
1½ cups heavy cream
2 tablespoons finely chopped parsley
    and chives

Cook the rice in the clam broth until very soft, about 45 minutes. Drain and reserve the broth.

Rub the rice through a fine sieve, and return to the broth. Chop the clams very fine. Or puree the rice and the clams together with a bit of broth in a blender or food processor. Combine the broth, rice, clams, and butter in a saucepan, and bring to the boiling point. Reduce the heat and simmer for 5 minutes. Season with salt and pepper to taste. Allow to cool. Then stir in the cream, and chill thoroughly. Serve in soup cups with a sprinkling of the chopped herbs.

SCALLOPED CLAMS

Serves 4

A satisfying dish that can be quickly prepared, especially if you are using canned minced clams, which works nicely in this case.

2 cups minced clams
½ cup butter, melted
½ cup toasted bread crumbs
1 cup cracker crumbs
Salt
Freshly ground black pepper
Paprika
2 tablespoons finely chopped onion
2 tablespoons finely chopped parsley
Additional butter
⅓ cup heavy cream

Mix the melted butter with the crumbs, and add a sprinkling of salt and pepper and a dash of paprika. Reserve one-third of this. Mix the rest with the clams, onion, and parsley. Place in a buttered baking dish, and top with the reserved buttered crumbs. Dot with additional butter, pour the cream over all, and bake at 375° for 20 to 25 minutes.

SCALLOPS AND OTHER SHELLFISH

BEARD ON SCALLOPS, MUSSELS, AND CRAYFISH

The scallop is named for its beautifully fluted shell. Two kinds are found in our waters—the tiny bay scallop and the much larger sea scallop. The bay scallop is tenderer, more delicate in flavor, and more sought after. Consequently it is less abundant. The sea scallop is widely available. What we call a scallop in this country is really only the muscle that controls the shell. (Europeans eat the whole creature.) One pound will amply feed 2 to 3 persons as a main course; 4, as an appetizer.

Mussels are found in profusion on both the East and West Coasts of the United States, yet they remain the most neglected of our seafoods, which cannot be entirely blamed on the fact that some Pacific Coast varieties are inedible during certain times of the year and must be quarantined. There are no such inhibitions in Europe where mussels are so popular that natural sources must be supplemented by artificial propagation. Certainly France has given us the most ubiquitous and most universally enjoyed mussel dish of all time—moules marinière.

When I was growing up in Oregon, we children organized fishing parties and would sit on the riverbanks and drag in crayfish by the dozen. Alas, in these days of industrial pollution and dirty streams, crayfish seem to have all but disappeared from our lives and our menus. Only rarely now do you get crayfish in the Pacific Northwest, although in Louisiana and the Delta country they are still eaten in quantities. The people of Sweden and other Scandinavian countries think so highly of crayfish that they hold annual festivals in August and feast on them with akvavit and beer. And they are the beloved *écrevisses* of the French. If you can find or order crayfish in your locality, they are something to hail with joy and treat with reverence.

SCALLOPS PROVENÇAL

Serves 6

This dish can be made with sea scallops cut into smaller pieces, but it is best made with tiny bay scallops.

1½ pounds bay scallops
Flour
6 tablespoons olive oil
2 or 3 cloves of garlic, finely
  chopped
Salt
Freshly ground black pepper
½ cup chopped parsley
Lemon wedges

Wash scallops and dry thoroughly. Lightly coat with flour, and shake off any excess. Heat the olive oil in a large skillet until quite hot, add the scallops and cook very quickly—only a minute or two, until they lose their translucent appearance. As soon as they begin to cook, add the garlic and a sprinkling of salt and pepper. Finally add the chopped parsley, and toss. Serve at once, plain or on fried toast, with lemon wedges.

SCALLOP QUICHE

Serves 4 to 6

Quiches made with a seafood filling are especially delicate, but no quiche can be successful unless the custard is cooked just to the right stage (better slightly underdone than overdone) and the bottom crust is crisp.

Pre-baked 9-inch pastry shell
1 to 1½ cups raw bay scallops or
    sea scallops cut in smaller pieces
1 to 1½ cups heavy cream
4 eggs
Salt and freshly ground black
    pepper to taste
Pinch of thyme
3 tablespoons crumbled crisp bacon

The pastry shell should be baked in a 425° oven for 15 to 20 minutes, until the bottom is set and the edges are slightly brown, then brushed with beaten egg yolk and baked for another 2 minutes to seal the crust. Arrange the scallops in the pastry. Blend the heavy cream and eggs together to make a custard mixture, season with salt and

pepper, and add the thyme and bacon. Pour over the scallops. Bake at 350° until the custard is barely set, about 30 minutes. A knife inserted at the center should come out clean. Do not overcook or the custard will curdle and become watery.

VARIATION:

Instead of the thyme and bacon, flavor the quiche with a teaspoon of chopped fresh dill, a teaspoon of onion juice, and 2 tablespoons of chopped parsley.

56

SEVICHE OF SCALLOPS

The fruit juice does the cooking in this traditional Latin-American appetizer.

1½ pounds bay scallops

1 cup fresh lime juice or half lime–half lemon juice

½ cup olive oil

2 tablespoons chopped canned green chilies

¼ cup chopped parsley

¼ cup finely sliced green onion

1 clove of garlic, finely chopped

1½ teaspoons salt

1 teaspoon freshly ground black pepper

Dash of Tabasco

1 tablespoon chopped fresh coriander

Put the scallops in a bowl, pour in the citrus juice, and refrigerate for 4 hours. The scallops will "cook" and turn opaque. Drain the scallops and combine with the olive oil, chopped chilies, parsley, green onions, garlic, and seasonings. Chill for another ½ hour. Transfer to a serving dish and sprinkle with chopped coriander. Serve with drinks or as a first course.

MOULES MARINIÈRE

Serves 4

This is probably the most popular of all mussel dishes, though sometimes made incorrectly. Here is an authentic recipe.

2 quarts mussels
1 large onion, chopped
2 cloves garlic, chopped
4 sprigs parsley
7 tablespoons butter
Salt, if needed
Freshly ground black pepper
1 cup white wine
2 tablespoons chopped parsley

Scrub and beard the mussels. Put the onion, garlic, and parsley sprigs into a heavy enameled or stainless steel pan. Add the mussels, 4 tablespoons of the butter, and a few grinds of pepper. Pour in the wine, cover the pan, and steam over low heat until the mussels open.

Arrange the mussels in a serving dish. Strain the broth through a linen cloth, and stir in the remaining butter and the chopped parsley. Taste for salt. Heat thoroughly, and pour over the mussels. Serve with French bread.

MUSSELS WITH SPINACH GRATINÉ

Serves 4

Mussels steamed Marinière style are the basis for a number of other dishes, this being one of the most interesting of them.

2 quarts mussels, steamed as for
    Moules Marinière
1½ cups cooked chopped spinach
Salt
Freshly ground black pepper
Mussel broth
1½ cups heavy cream
Beurre manié
Buttered bread crumbs
½ cup grated Swiss cheese

Shell the mussels. Season the chopped spinach to taste, and combine with the mussels. Heat the strained mussel broth with the heavy cream, and thicken with *beurre manié* (pea-sized balls of butter and flour). Mix the sauce with the mussels and spinach. Spoon into a buttered baking dish. Top with buttered crumbs and sprinkle with the grated cheese. Bake at 425° until the cheese melts and the crumbs are slightly browned.

STUFFED MUSSELS PROVENÇAL

Serves 4

The mussels can be prepared as for Moules Marinière (see p. 58) before stuffing, instead of being steamed in plain water.

2 quarts mussels
6 shallots, finely chopped
2 cloves, finely chopped
½ cup chopped parsley
1 teaspoon salt
½ teaspoon freshly ground black pepper
1 egg yolk
½ cup bread crumbs
½ pound butter, slightly softened
White wine

Wash and beard the mussels. Steam them, covered, in a deep kettle with a little water until they open. Allow them to cool. Remove the empty half of each shell.

Mix the shallots, garlic, parsley, seasonings, egg yolk, and bread crumbs, and blend thoroughly into the butter. Spoon some of this mixture over each mussel in its half-shell. Arrange in a baking pan, and pour a little white wine around the mussels. Bake in a 400° oven just until the stuffing is delicately browned.

CRAYFISH BORDELAISE

Serves 4

One of the simplest and most delicious ways to cook these succulent shellfish.

36 to 40 crayfish
2 carrots, finely diced
2 ribs celery, finely diced
2 onions, finely chopped
5 tablespoons butter
Salt
Freshly ground black pepper
2 cups dry white wine
1½ cups tomato puree or tomato
   sauce

Wash the crayfish, and tear off the tiny wing in the center of the tail to extract the intestine. Melt the butter in a large kettle, add the vegetables, and cook over low heat until they are softened. Season with salt and pepper. Add the wine and let it cook down for a few minutes. Then add the crayfish, and cook just until the shells turn red, about 5 minutes. Mix in the tomato puree, and bring to a boil. Correct the seasoning. Pour into a large tureen. Serve with saffron rice, a green salad, and crisp bread.

ARTICHOKES STUFFED WITH SHELLFISH

The artichokes can be served either hot or cold—stuffed with creamed shellfish, if hot; with shellfish salad, if cold.

1 large artichoke per serving
For the filling, use any one of the following:

> *Creamed oysters, creamed mixed seafood, lobster salad, mixed seafood salad, mussel salad*

Cut off the spiny tip of each leaf. Remove any discolored outer leaves. Cut the stem end flush with the bottom so it will stand upright. Cook the artichokes in boiling acidulated water until just tender, about 40 minutes. A leaf will pull out easily when done. Drain the artichokes upside down. When cooled, remove the choke from each and the center leaves.

If they are to be served hot, reheat in a steamer over hot water. If they are to be served cold, chill in the refrigerator. Fill hot artichokes with creamed oysters or creamed mixed seafood. Fill cold artichokes with lobster salad, mixed seafood salad, or mussel salad.

SEAFOOD QUICHES

Serves 4 to 6

Also see the Scallop Quiche on p. 56 for another seafood variation.

Pre-baked 9-inch pastry shell
1 to 1½ cups heavy cream
4 eggs, lightly beaten
Salt
Freshly ground black pepper

FOR LOBSTER QUICHE:
1½ cups cooked lobster meat.
Flavor with any one of the following:
    tarragon, cognac and paprika,
    sherry, Madeira.

FOR CRAB QUICHE:
½ pound of cooked crabmeat.
Flavor with any one of the following:
    finely chopped onion, parsley
    and green pepper; fresh dill; tar-
    ragon and parsley; chives and
    parsley; sherry; Madeira.

FOR SHRIMP QUICHE:
1 to 1½ cups cooked shrimp, cut into
    small pieces.
Flavor with any of the following:
    fresh dill; fresh or dried tarragon;
    a touch of curry powder blended
    with the custard; 1 teaspoon chili
    powder; 1 or 2 canned green chilies,
    chopped; sherry or cognac and
    paprika; 2 tablespoons lightly
    sautéed onion, 2 tablespoons
    tomato paste, 1 small clove garlic,
    finely chopped, and 2 tablespoons
    chopped parsley.

Blend the cream with the eggs and salt and pepper to taste. Stir in any liquid flavoring. Spread the seafood in the pre-baked pastry shell, add any other flavoring of your choice, and pour in the custard. Bake in a 350° oven until the custard is set, about 30 minutes.

SHELLFISH PANCAKES

Use your favorite pancake batter for this recipe, omitting the sugar, or follow the basic one given here.

1 cup minced clams, drained; or 1 cup cooked shrimp, finely chopped; or 1 cup flaked cooked crabmeat
Salt
Freshly ground black pepper
Chopped fresh herbs to taste—dill, tarragon, chives, or parsley (optional)

FOR THE PANCAKES:
2 cups sifted all-purpose flour
4 teaspoons baking powder
1 teaspoon salt
2 eggs, lightly beaten
1½ cups milk
¼ cup melted butter

Season the shellfish well with salt and pepper. Prepare the pancake batter: Sift the dry ingredients together. Combine the eggs, milk, and butter. Stir into the dry ingredients until the large lumps disappear. Then gently stir in the shellfish and herbs.

Drop the batter by spoonfuls on a hot, lightly greased griddle to make cakes about 4 inches in diameter. When bubbles form on the surface and the edges seem cooked, turn and lightly brown on the other side. Serve with a sprinkling of chopped parsley and a tartar sauce.